Naughty Adult Joke Book

#3

Dirty, Funny and Slutty Jokes That Make Japanese Sashimi Smell Bad

Jason S. Jones

Naughty Adult Joke Book:
Dirty, Slutty, Funny Jokes That Broke The Censors

Why is a vagina similar to bad weather?

Once it wets, you have to go in.

READ NOW ON AMAZON

Naughty Adult Joke Book #7:
Dirty, Funny And Slutty Jokes That Should Never Be Said In Bed

What makes the cock different from the paycheck?

You never have to beg your wife to blow the paycheck.

READ NOW ON AMAZON.COM

Table of Contents

Introduction

Congratulations on downloading the *Naughty Adult Joke Book: Dirty, Funny and Slutty Jokes That Make Japanese Sashimi Smell Bad* and thank you for doing so. There exists a myth that the Japanese are a tough crowd; that they do not tell jokes to each other; that they do not laugh at jokes. Well, while there could be an ounce of truth to that, the reality is that the Japanese are happy people, very proper and cultured, but they also have a naughty streak to them.

Reading this book, you will discover that there is a 'pun' in Ja-pan! The Japanese also have a variety of very naughty adult jokes that, well, could make Japanese Sashimi smell bad. There is a variety of good-natured sex jokes, jokes about Japanese technology, some funny puns, and other jokes designed to tickle the adult mind.

Adult jokes do not make you a dirty person. Everyone has a dirty thought pop up one time or the other, and we are not perverts! Therefore, read this book with confidence. Chuckle here and there, roll on the floor with laughter, and have your ribs hurting. Life is short, and we need to spend every minute happy, sometimes with the help of a unique adult book like this one. Go ahead, brighten up your day, and your life!

To that end, the jokes are divided into two sections: The short and the long jokes. The short jokes are puns, one-liners, and short Q&As. The second section contains long jokes. They are excellent too because they provide context for the joke, so you see the funny in each situation. It is said that laughter prolongs life; with this book, you just might live forever!

There are plenty of books on this subject on the market, so thanks again for choosing this one! Every effort was made to ensure it is full of as much useful information as possible. Please, enjoy!

Chapter 1: Jokes and Punch Lines

Section 1: Short Jokes

Q: How do all Japanese jokes begin?

A: They begin when you look over your shoulder.

Q: How many Japanese people would you need to screw a light bulb?

A: It doesn't really matter because they all are too short.

Q: What name is given to a Japanese woman who only has one leg?

A: Irene

Q: At what time did the Godzilla eat the Prime Minister of Japan?

A: Eight P.M.

Q: What is the favorite holiday for a Japanese girl?

A: 'Erection' Day

Q: What is the reason behind all Asian girls having small boobs?

A: In Asia, only A's are acceptable.

Q: Why was Jesus not born in Japan?

A: The angels could not trace any virgin nor wise man.

Q: What has a halo and two wings?

A: A Japanese telephone: Wing wing, halo?

Q: Suppose a horse and a pig were in a race, which of them would win?

A: The pig (Why? "Ton-katsu da kara." "Ton-katsu" is pork cutlet, and the "katsu" means "to win.")

Q: What name a Japanese protest called?

A: A SITUASIAN

Q: Now that Japanese pop is sometimes called JPOP, what name is given to Chinese rap?

A: CRAP!

Q: How do you get a one-armed man from on top of a tree?

A: Wave

Q: Why can't you find any Japanese bingo players?

A: The players disappear upon hearing B-29

Q: What was the girl told by her Japanese father?

A: You say you're allergic to bees? You had better be. You either get As on your report card or C your way out of my house!

Q: What do Japanese kids eat during snack time?
A: Anime Crackers

Q: What do they eat for breakfast in Tokyo?
A: Japancakes

Q: If a group of Asians are in a pool, what do you call that?
A: Rice Krispies

A lady and her lover are on a motel bed going at it good when suddenly, the lady exclaims, "You know what I'm doing is strictly against the doctor's orders." "What is the matter honey, are you ill?" "No, I am married to a doctor."

Q: What do you suppose is the difference between a unicorn and a smart Japanese man?
A: Nothing — both are fictional characters

Q: How would you tell if a Japanese gang had robbed your house?
A: All the rice in the house would be gone, and you still would find the robbers trying to back the car out of the driveway

Q: What made the Japanese Kamikaze pilot fly the plane back to base?

A: He had forgotten his helmet.

Q: What leads the Japanese Sumo wrestlers to shave the hairs on their legs?
A: So that others can tell them apart from the feminists.

Q: What name is given to a Hiroshima citizen?
A: A rice crispy.

Q: Which is the best way to punish a blind man?
A: By rearranging the furniture.

Q: Suppose a Japanese ship sinks and only one lifeboat is available, how many people would be saved?
A: Nine (In Japanese, a lifeboat is called a 'kyuu-mei,' and this is also another way of saying 'nine people').

Q: How would you blindfold an Asian?
A: Dental floss.

Q: What do Asians do when they have an erection?
A: They vote.

Q: Why did the mermaid wear seashells?
A: Her boobs were too big for the B-shells.

Q: How do you know whether an ant is a male or a female?

A: They would call them uncles if they were male.

Q: Why did the gangsta sit under the tree?

A: Because it is shady.

Q: What name do you give to a belt with a watch on it?

A: A waist of time.

Q: Why do thieves have such a hard time understanding sarcasm?

A: They take things literally.

Q: What do you call a pile of cats?

A: A meowtain.

Q: What is the Buddhism unit of measure?

A: Oooooohms

Q: Suppose a Japanese mugger approached you, what would he say?

A: "Give me all your money or I'll kill myself."

Q: What does a Japanese bakery thief say?

A: I Tokyo cookie

Q: What do you call a homeless guy in Japan?

A: A Tokyo drifter

Q: Why did James Brown always tour in Asia?

A: He loved the Seoul train.

Q: What did the handless guy get for Christmas?

A: It's still a mystery because he hasn't opened his present yet.

Q: What do you get when you punch Batman in the groin?

A: A bruised wang.

Doctor: I have some sad news for you; your kidneys are failing.

Me: Oh no… Why is this happening?

Wife (Sobbing): How shall we break this news to our son?

Me: Leave that to me… I will tell him.

(Later on. . . sitting with our son at home)

Me: I have some bad news son. Your knees are failing.

Shintoism: I mean, a reverence for spirits, nature, and ancestors with no formal dogma? Get real Japan.

I had sex with a Japanese man once. It was great. He made me origami three times.

Dark humor is like free healthcare. Not everybody gets it.

Whenever a guy doesn't share my sense of humor, I tell them that my jokes are a lot like blowjobs. You don't get them.

A girl having 12 boobs sounds weird. Dozen tit?

Bullets are so weird. They only do their job after they are fired.

My girlfriend dumped me because I have a weird nickname for my penis. I guess I have to take Matter into my own hands.

Internet humor is so selfish. It's all about meme meme meme.

My dad was trying to explain what sarcasm is the other day and I couldn't understand what he was saying. All I remember is him telling me that he loved me.

I would love to tell a joke about Buddhism, but I don't have enough karma.

My grandpa survived both the Nagasaki and Hiroshima bombings! Being in Australia helped.

She had a photographic memory that was never developed.

The most efficient way to ensure that you never forget your wife's birthday is to forget it one time!

Backed up into the meat grinder, the butcher got a little behind on the orders.

A Japanese guy walks into a supermarket to buy chicken. However, he didn't know how to pronounce "chicken." He walks over to the aisle, grabs an egg, walks off to an attendant and demands, "Where is the mother?"

He always broke into song because he couldn't find the key.

A small Japanese-bred dog taking a walk with his owner bit a man. The owner got his shitzued out of him!

Men have wisened up and realized that it's cheaper to marry the girl and keep her home than only date her but take her out.

If you spun around a Japanese man, would he become disoriented?

Which is the most effective pregnancy test in Japan? An unsolved Rubik's cube is inserted into the lady's vagina, and if it comes out solved, she is pregnant!

Why did the teacher wear sunglasses? Because her students were so bright!

How do you tell if an Asian's eyes are open or closed? You can't!

They finally came up with a generic name for over-the-counter Viagra: Mycoxaflopin

Ten puns got into the annual comedy contest in their town. At the end, a man from the audience asked, "So, who won?" The judge answered, "No pun in ten did."

A dentist and manicurist fought tooth and nail.

I have decided to write all of my jokes in capitals from now on… This one was taken in Tokyo.

I arranged a threesome on the weekend. Had two no shows, but I still had fun.

Jokes about homosexuals are not funny. I mean, come on, guys!

I'll never date another apostrophe. The last one was too possessive.

Avoid dangerous cults. Practice safe sects.

I asked my wife why she married me. She said, "Because you are quite funny." I said, "I thought it was because I was good in bed. Wife chuckles, "You see? That's hilarious."

Vandals have broken into The National Origami Museum in Tokyo. Stay tuned to receive more news as the story unfolds.

Being vegan is a bit of a cult: They just egg each other on!

My comedian friend arranged a date with a girl and didn't show up.
Naturally, she wasn't pleased.
Some people just don't appreciate stand-up comedy these days.

Another Tsunami has hit Japan. The city of Tokyo is now covered in seaweed and fish. One newspaper described the situation as delicious.

Two guys are driving along a street in the city when they see a dog on the side of the road licking his penis. "I sure wish I could do that," one guy says. The other replies, "But, don't you think you ought to pet him first?"

I informed my wife that, from today, I was going to start smoking pot. She said if I did, she would leave me. I guess it's true what they say… Marijuana truly is an effective way of getting rid of pains and aches.

Boss: Sarcasm will get you nowhere in life!
Me: Well, it got me to the International Sarcasm finals in Santiago in 2012.
Boss: Really?
Me: No

Two Asian immigrants have just arrived in the United States and they can't help but compare the United States to their home country. One of them talks about a rumor he heard about Americans: They eat dogs! He insists that if they are going to fit in, they had better learn how to eat dogs also. Taking that suggestion, the two walk to a hotdog stand and make an order for two "dogs". As the first unwraps his meal, he nervously looks at his friend, "What part did you get?"

In 1868, Japan moved its seat of government and the location of its Emperor's home from Kyoto to Tokyo.
It wasn't a big deal; they merely did some rearrangement and changed the capital letter.

Next time your wife is angry, drape a towel over her shoulders…
…and say, "Now you're super angry."

Maybe she laughs;

Maybe you die.

Standing in front of an airline ticket agent, I made my request. I said, "I want to buy a ticket to London, but I want one bag to go to Tokyo and the other to Moscow."

"Sir, we can't do that," the ticket agent exclaimed.

"Why not?" I asked. "You did it to me last time I flew with you."

In Japan, it is not enough to want something really badly, you have to want it so much 'your hand comes out of your mouth.'

In Japan, you do not just grow tired of hearing something said to you repeatedly, you grow so tired that callouses grow on your ears.

In a situation in which you can do nothing about, in Japan, you are not just helpless; you are 'a carp on a cutting board.'

A small amount is not just a pittance, in Japan, it is a 'sparrow's tear.'

In Japan, fear does not just paralyze you, it turns you into a 'frog glared at by a snake.'

In Japan, a person who can help you in a desperate situation is not just a savior; the person is your 'Buddha in hell.'

In Japan, you are not just honest in your speech, you 'speak with your belly cut open.'

In Japan, you do not just say that you are very, very busy, you say that 'you're so busy you could borrow a cat's paw.'

In Japan, you do not just take a quick bath, you must 'shower like a crow.'

When something confusing and unexpected happens to a Japanese, he feels 'tricked by a fox'.

In Japan, when somebody is respectable and worthy of your respect, you do not just take him as your mentor and follow in his footsteps; you 'brew and drink the dirt after the individual's nails.'

In Japan, when something is really small, you do not just say it's "tiny". You say, "It is the size of a cat's forehead."

In Japan, you do not just love your child or grandchild to bits, you say that 'it wouldn't hurt even if you were to put that person right in your eye.'

If someone stands in your way, in Japan, he is not just in your way, he is a 'lump above your eye.'

If you eat something delicious in Japan, you say that the food item is so good 'your cheeks are falling off.'

If you know of someone who has never had to work hard in life because he has had an easy life, you can describe the person as one who has 'never had to lift anything heavier than chopsticks.'

If a story does not have a clear ending and is unfinished, it is called 'a dragonfly whose tail is cut off.'

If you operate a restaurant or a shop in Japan and business is slow, you say, "The cuckoos are crying."

When two people hate each other in Japan, they are said to have a 'monkey and dog' relationship.

In Japan, when doing a comparison between two things that are entirely different, you don't just plainly say that there is no comparison, you say, "It's like comparing the moon and a soft-shelled turtle."

I heard that Chinese opium is so strong it can kill you. No wonder it's a drug for youth-in-Asia.

You cannot Tokyo Drift in a Tesla; you can only do the Electric Slide.

An old man sat outside a pub trying to fish in a puddle. A well-dressed gentleman passing by thought, "Poor old fool." However, he invited the old man inside the pub for a drink. As they sipped their drinks, the gentleman thought he would humor the old man and asked, "So, how many have you caught today?"
"You're the eighth," the old man replied.

The biggest Catholic news now is that the Pope declared that there stood a chance for atheists to go to Heaven. One thing he didn't make clear, however, is that once they get there, they would spend eternity helping Buddha squeeze into his yoga pants.

My boss fired me for making too many Asian jokes.
It was the end of my Korea.
I'm still China find another job.

On average, the American adult male has sex two to three times every week, while a Japanese adult male has sex once or twice in a year. This is upsetting news to me because I had no idea I was Japanese.

They just announced that in the next *Fast and Furious* movie, the cast will be going undercover as ride share drivers in Asia. It is called "Tokyo Lift".

A kid asked his mom, "Mom, what is dark humor?"
The mom responded, "See that man over there with no arms? Tell him to clap."
Kid: "But mom, I'm blind!"
Mom: "Exactly!"

Section 2: Long Jokes

A Japanese sewage worker has finished his day's work and met up with his friends at a local bar in Tokyo. They get to talking about their different jobs, and one of the friends remarks, "It must be hard work doing what you do — I don't think I could stand the smell!"

"Oh, yeah, it's pretty bad," the sewage worker replies.

"What about the guys you work with, are they good people?" another asks.

"To tell you the truth," the sewage worker answers, "I don't really know; it's so dark down there, I can't even see them. We just pass like nips in the shit."

A man goes to a hospital, concerned about a wound in his groin. The doctor asks him, "Whoa! What happened to you?"

The man answers, "I was taking a class on gun safety. I've never used a gun before, and wanted to learn how to correctly use one. It didn't go over well."

The doctor was puzzled. "I see that. Well, what happened? Did someone else misfire?

The man replied, "Well, not exactly. It all happened when the instructor asked us to cock out guns."

Jerking Off

A waitress at a New York City restaurant walks up to a table to find three Japanese men. She surprisingly finds that the three of them are furiously masturbating.

"What the hell are you perverts doing?" she furiously asks, to which one of the three replies, "We all berry hungry!"

"But why are you jerkin' off?" Another of the three responds, "Because menu say, "First come, first served!"

The Bear and the Rabbit

A bear and a rabbit are both in the bush, taking a shit. The bear having finished his business, turns to the rabbit and asks, "Do you mind if shit sticks to your fur?" "No, I don't mind at all," the rabbit replies. The bear moves over and runs his ass all over the rabbit, spreading the shit all over him.

The Woman Created

One day, Adam approached God with a question.

"God, why did you make Eve so beautiful?" God answered, "So you would love her."

Adam went on to ask, "Lord, why did you make her feel so soft and nice?" "So, you would love her," The Lord answered.

"But why would you make her so dumb?" Adam probed. "So, she would love you."

The Disciplinarian Japanese Father

A Japanese father was feeling frustrated and started venting. He said, "When I was a young boy, my parents disciplined me by sending me to my room without supper, but in my son's room, he has his own telephone, smart TV, and computer."

"So, what do you do?" his mate enquired.

"I send him to MY room!" the father exclaimed.

The Blind Fold

An American guy sat outside his favorite restaurant in Atlanta city when a Japanese fellow sitting across him approached him, saying, "I am sick of your big round eyes."

"Put on a blind fold," retorted the American guy.

"Where do I get one?" Asked the Japanese guy.

"Here," the American answered, "Have my shoe lace."

Mitsubishi

An older woman is at the checkout point at a grocery store. She begins to take notice of the bag-boy and her sexual desires begin to soar.

Once she has paid for her groceries, she walks behind the bag-boy as he is carrying her bags to the parking lot. In her mind, she is working out a plan on how to seduce him.

On getting outside the store, the old woman leans over and whispers in the boy's ear, "I have an itchy pussy."

The boy is concerned and answers, "Well, you will have to point it out… All these Japanese cars look the same."

After Studying Different Religions

After studying various religions, here is what I found:

Christianity is too cross

Buddhism kept repeating itself

Islam kept dropping bombs on me

Judaism made my hair curl

Hinduism made me have a cow

Japanese Men Getting Better At Sex

The Japanese men have figured out sex. One man, after nights of unlucky attempts to seduce his wife, he finally came up with a proposition that he presented to her. He said to her, "If you are in the mood to have sex with me, let me know by pulling on my penis just once." He continued, "However if you are not in the mood, let me know by pulling on my penis 100 times."

The American Businessman

An American businessman met with the managers from his company's Japanese location in Tokyo. On his first night in town, he arranged to have a hooker come up to his room at the hotel. As they engaged in sex, the hooker kept squirming and moaning, "Sung wa! Sung wa!" The American, not understanding Japanese, assumed that the hooker was only having a good time and assumed that 'Sung wa!" was an expression of pleasure.

The next day, the man and his three managers decided to go playing golf, and I the middle of a round, one of the managers shot a hole in one. The American shouted excitedly, "Sung wa! Sung wa!"

The Japanese manager turned to his boss and asked, "Wrong hole? You mean it's the wrong hole?"

The Negligent Discharge

A duck hunter is in the forest enjoying a quiet morning out in marsh when he decides to take a piss. He walks to a nearby tree and props his gun against the tree. Unfortunately, a strong gust of wind starts to blow and the gun falls over, gets discharged, shoots him squarely in the groin area.

Some hours pass and the man finds himself lying on a hospital bed. A doctor approaches him. "Well, sir, I have both good and bad news. The good news is that you're going to be okay. The damage to your groin was local, there was very little internal damage. We were able to take out all the buckshot."

Pleased by the report, the hunter goes on to ask, "Now, what's the bad news?"

"The bad news is that there was some nasty buckshot damage done to your penis. I'm going to have to refer you to my brother."

"Oh, well, I guess it's not that bad," the hunter responded. "Is your brother a plastic surgeon?"

"No, not at all." The doctor answered. "He plays the flute at the local symphony, and he will teach you where to put your fingers so you don't piss in your eye."

The Intensive Care in Japan

There was a case in one of Japan's hospitals where the attendants noticed that patients from placed on a particular bed always died, regardless of their medical condition. The time of death would always be 11 a.m. on Sunday morning. Puzzled, some doctors even suggested that this had to do with something supernatural. But why death?

Being the scientists, they are, the doctors decided to investigate the cause of the incidents, before concluding that something supernatural was involved. So, the next Sunday, at 11 o'clock in the morning, all the nurses and doctors were standing at a corner in the ward, waiting to see what was causing the unfortunate occurrences. They gathered there with their prayer books, rosaries, crosses and any other holy object they could find, with the intention of warding off any evil that would show up.

Immediately, as the clock struck 11, in walked Sooki, the part-time sweeper who came in on Sundays entered the ward and unplugged the life support system to make room for his vacuum cleaner.

The Cheating Husband

A woman comes to the knowledge that her husband has been cheating on her. She immediately hires a hitman to enact the ultimate revenge.

When the two meet up, the woman explains through her rage, that she wants the hitman to shoot the other woman in the head, and, wanting her husband to suffer too, she asks that he be shot in the groin, enough to punish him, but not to kill him.

As expected, that evening, the husband was meeting up with his mistress. The wife also was meeting up with the hitman at the top of a hill that they hoped would give them a vantage point. The hill was behind the wife's house.

The mistress finally showed up, and the hitman, through the scope of his sniper rifle, could see the union between the mistress and the cheating husband. Relaying these details to the wife, the wife began to instruct him, "Come on! Get on with it! Shoot his dick off and blow her brains out!"

After a short pause, the hitman says, "Hold on… I think I can get it all in one shot."

It Works!

A woman is walking through the park when she comes across a man looking rather sad and depressed in his wheelchair. The woman, concerned to know what is bothering the man, asks, "What is wrong?"

The man looks at her with his sad eyes, points to his groin and shaking his head says, "I just want to have sex, but…"

The woman interjects, "Oh, I understand. Well, tell you what, I'd like to do something for you." The woman takes the man back to her apartment and begins riding him hard. The man is completely aroused and he slides it in and begins to do her with an elated expression. In the middle of it, when the pleasure is too much, the man starts screaming, "It works! It works! It works!" Perplexed, the lady asks, "Your penis?"

"No!" the man answers her, "Pretending to be disabled to get laid works!"

The Quality of Japanese Products

The people at IBM are still laughing at this. Apparently, the computer manufacturing giant, IBM, decided to have some of its parts made in Japan as a way to test a new production strategy. In their specifications, the company clearly indicated that it would only allow a maximum of three defective parts in every 10,000 parts.

When the time of delivery came, the goods came in with an accompanying letter reading, "We, Japanese people have a hard time understanding the business practices of the North American business persons. Therefore, we produced the three defective parts that you requested per 10,000 parts. We manufactured them separately and included them in this consignment. We hope that this will please you."

The Physical Therapist

Two ladies were playing golf when one of their balls flew off, landing on one of the men playing at the next hole. In pain, the man gripped his hands together put them on his groin, dropped to the ground, and began to roll as he reeled in pain and agony.

Seeing this, the woman who had swung her club rushed to see the man and to apologize. "Please allow me to help. I am a physical therapist, and I could help to relieve your pain if only you would let me," she said.

"Oh no. I'll be alright in a few minutes," the man replied, trying to be brave. Everyone could see that he was in great pain as he lay there, in fetal position, with his hands still tightly clasped and buried in his groin.

The woman continued to insist that she could help, and, driven by her persistence, the man finally gave in.

She picked his hands gently, away from the groin area, put them on his sides, slackened his pants, and slid her hands into the pants. She gave him some artful tender massage for several minutes before turning to her patient to ask, "How does that feel?"

The man replied, "It feels great, but I think my thumb's still broken."

The Ass That Cried Honda

An American auto parts supplier sent his sales rep to an important meeting in Tokyo to meet with the Toyota chairman to close a huge deal. On getting to his hotel, the sales rep farted, and, strangely, he heard the fart sound like his ass was saying "Honda." Puzzled, the sales rep forced out another fart, and this time, also, the ass sounded "Hooonda." As you would expect, the sales rep was petrified by these events. The rest of the evening, whenever he farted, the same 'Hoooonda' sound came out.

Flipping through his phone later that night, the man found an American doctor's contacts and rushed over. The doctor took time to listen to the bizarre farts, gave him a thorough examination, then finally declared that he was completely baffled.

The doctor referred to the sales rep to a Japanese doctor who specializes in rare diseases, but the new doctor did not have a clue, also. He immediately booked the sales rep for an emergency examination by a gastroenterologist. The specialist was stumped, too. Needless to say, on his way out the last doctor's office, the man was beyond panicking. He decided to cancel out the meeting he had with the Toyota chairman the next day. He figured that it would be totally embarrassing if, while seated in the chairman's office, a fart slipped and came out screaming 'Hoooonda!"

Just before the sales rep closed the door behind him, however, the doctor's receptionist recommended that he ought to go see a dentist. What the heck? A dentist? What would a dentist have to do with his digestive tract?

Anyway, at this time, the man was desperate, and he didn't have a choice at this time. He decided to oblige and booked a session with a local dentist.

When he arrived, despite seeing the bizarrely of his visit, the sales rep explained his problem to the old Japanese dentist. All the while, the dentist kept nodding. When the guy was done explaining his case, the dentist said to him, "You have an abscessed tooth.

"An abscessed tooth?" the skeptical sales rep wondered. "Why the hell would you conclude that?"

The dentist replied, "Everyone knows that abscess makes the fart go 'Honda'."

Nelson Mandela

Nelson Mandela is seated at his couch watching TV when he hears a knock on the door. He rises to open it and finds a Japanese delivery man clutching his clipboard. The delivery guy points to a truck on the driveway that is packed full of car exhausts, and excitedly starts indicating to Mandela, "You sign! You sign!"

The President is bewildered, and slams the door in the delivery guy's face. He will do no such thing.

The next day, the delivery guy is back, and the events of the previous day are repeated. Again, he waves the clipboard in Mandela's face and points to a truckload of brake pads and insists, "You sign! You sign!" Again, Nelson will have none of it and sends the guy away.

The next day, the guy is back with two truckloads of car parts, and again, he is insisting that the president signs the clipboard. At this time, Mandela is already losing his temper and he shouts, "Look, I don't want these. Do you understand? You have the wrong address."

The man is puzzled. He looks at his clipboard and back at Mandela, "You not Nissan Main dealer?"

Stevie Wonder

Stevie Wonder is in Tokyo for his first gig and, as expected, the venue is packed to the rafters. However, since Stevie has never been to Japan, he decides to ask for a special request that could break the ice with his new audience.

From the first row jumps a little old Japanese man shouting at the top of his voice… "Play a jazz chord! Play a jazz chord!"

Stevie perceives that this old guy understands the great influence that jazz had in growing Stevie's career, and rising to the challenge and being one to impress, Stevie begins to play an E minor scale, then moves on to a more difficult jazz melody that goes on for about 10 minutes. On finishing, the place goes wild.

The little man at the front jumps up again and shouts, "No, no! Play a jazz chord! Play a jazz chord!"

At this time, Stevie is perplexed, but being the professional he is, he goes on to improvise a jazz sound with the help of his band. They play the B flat minor, and this time literally bring the house down. The crowd is blown away by this display of expertise. Everyone has now gone wild.

Again, the little man at the front is not satisfied. He jumps up again, climbs up the stage and grabs the microphone. He sings, "A jazz chord, to say, I ruv you…"

The Unfaithful Firefighter

A firefighter's wife has a hunch that her husband is getting some on the side. Being the non-confrontational type, she keeps quiet about it and is on a mission to prove, beyond doubt, that her husband is cheating on her.

One day, going through the content on her husband's glove box in the car, she comes across a packet of unused condoms. Smiling knowingly, the wife heads out to the house, soaks the condoms in some jalapeno for an hour, then puts them back in the car.

Later that night, the husband wakes up and announces that he is off to put out some fire. A half hour later, the husband is back home breathing fire. Under his breath, he also mumbles something about an inferno in his groin. He rushes from the kitchen carrying a bucket of ice and dumps it all on his crotch, all the while screaming blue murder.

A few moments later, the wife's BFF calls her and on the other end, she is hysterical, talking about how her nether regions have been invaded by a legion of fiery demons.

A Date with a Stunning Blonde

A guy got lucky because the blonde he was interested in agreed to go out on a date with him. While he was getting ready for the dinner date, he looked into the mirror and thought, "I should get some color! I know a safe place to get a tan on my roof."

That day, the sun was blazing hot. Nevertheless, the guy went to the roof, undressed completely, and decided to have a 30-minute tan. Unfortunately, the guy fell asleep. He was woken by a stinging itch and pain in the groin region. He had been badly burned. Unlucky for him, he only had an hour before the date, which meant that he could not get to a hospital for first aid.

Putting on his clothes, the guy drove off to the blonde's house, and fast forward, they were having sex. Soon after he came, the sunburn began to act up. The pain continued to escalate and, at some point, it became unbearable. The guy excused himself, saying he was going to get a drink in the kitchen.

When he opened the fridge, the guy took out a bottle of wine and two cartons of milk and juice. It was all that was there, anyway. Frantically, he doused his crotch with the wine and felt some relief. However, a minute later, the pain was up again. The man grabbed the juice and poured it onto his manhood.

At this time, the blonde, who was wondering what was taking the man so long, went to the kitchen just in time to see the man take out the milk and spill it on his piece.

Impressed, the blonde chuckled and remarked, "So that's how you refill it!"

The Female Gorilla

A while back, a zoo bought a female gorilla, and recently, the gorilla went in heat. The zookeeper phoned all his fellow keepers from different zoos to help find a male gorilla that could settle the issue in different zoos. The zookeeper called, called, and called, but the budget the board had accorded him to transport the gorilla was only $10,000. Unfortunately, none of his friends were willing to ship the male gorilla for ten grand only. On the ground, however, the gorilla was getting dangerously horny.

During one of the late nights at the zoo, the zookeeper, after making yet another series of unsuccessful calls to his friends in Tokyo, steps outside and sees the Janitor, Steven, sweeping around the gorilla's enclosure.

He says to him, "Steven, look, would you ever be interested in fucking this gorilla for ten grand?"

Steven looks at the zookeeper and appears to be in deep thought. After a minute or so, he says that he would be willing to, but he had three ground rules.

The first rule was that he would not be kissing the gorilla. The second rule was that no one would ever find out about this arrangement. The third rule was that he would need a few more days to bring the ten grand together.

The Bad Case of Small Cox

A young newlywed couple walks into their honeymoon suite. As they are undressing, stealing glances at each other, the bride notices the groom take his socks off, revealing some ungodly gnarly growths on his toes.

She immediately asks him what those are, to which he replies, "When I was a small boy, I had a bad case of tolio."

The bride retorts, "Don't you mean polio?"

"Nope, tolio." He replies.

The man proceeds to take off his pants and the bride is stunned to see some other huge growths on the groom's knees. She sought to know what had caused that.

"When I was little, I had a bad case of kneasles," the groom replies.

"Don't you mean measles" the bride replies.

"Nope, they were kneasles!"

At last, the groom pulls down his drawers. The bride looks intently at him. "Crap, I guess you also had a bad case of small cox!"

The Currency Exchange

A Japanese man is in New York City, and he walks into a currency exchange bureau. He hands over a wad of notes, 2000 yen, and he is handed 72 dollars in exchange. The next week, he walks in with yet another 2000 yen, and, in exchange, is given $66. Appalled, the man turns to the teller and asks why he received less money than he got the first time around.

"Fluctuations," The teller replies.

The Japanese man storms out the bureau, and just before he slammed the door, he turned around and shouted, "Fluc you Amelicans, too!"

The Fly and the Three Samurai

In an empire far away, the Emperor advertised that he wanted to hire a new Chief Samurai. A year later, only three people had submitted their applications: A Chinese, a Japanese and a Jewish Samurai. The Emperor asked them to demonstrate their skills.

The first applicant was the Japanese Samurai. He came up and flipped open a tiny box, letting out a fly. He then drew out his katana and… *Swish*, the fly fell down to the floor, neatly divided into two halves. The Emperor marveled. "What a feat!" he said.

Next came the Chinese Samurai. He bowed and took a step forward. He also flipped open the tiny box, released a fly, and, *swish, swash*, the fly fell to the floor in neat quarters. The Emperor was impressed by this, also. "That is skill!" he remarked.

Turning to the Jewish Samurai, the emperor asked him, "How are you going to top that?" Undeterred, the Jewish Samurai stepped forward, unlocked the tiny box in his hand, released the fly in it and drew his katana. *Swooooooooosh*, the katana went, and a breeze followed it, filling the entire room. However, the fly was still buzzing, moving from corner to corner.

The emperor was disappointed and angrily inquired, "What kind of skill is that? The fly isn't even dead."

"Dead, schmead," the Jewish Samurai replies. "Dead is easy. Circumcision… that takes skill!"

The Foreigner

A man immigrated from Japan to America. Since he couldn't speak English, he felt that mingling with the Americans would give him a shot at learning English faster. One afternoon, he joined a choir in a church, and by the end of their practice session, he could say, "Me me me me me me me."

The Japanese man went into the store and found a little girl who said, "He stole my dolly."

Walking home, the Japanese man into a butchery to buy meat, and from his interaction with the butcher, he grasped the words 'Big butcher knife, big butcher knife.'

On getting home, there came up an air freshener commercial on TV and from watching it, he learned to say the words 'Plug it in, Plug it in'

The next day, the man walked into the store, and unbeknownst to him, a man had been killed there. The police officer asked, "Who killed this man?"

The Japanese man answered, “Me me me me me me.”

The police were perplexed. “Why did you kill him?” he asked.

“He stole my dolly.”

“What did you kill him with?”

“Big butcher knife, Big butcher knife.”

The police officers took hold of the man and escorted him to the electric chair.

The police officer asked, “Any last words?”

The man said, “Plug it in, plug it in.”

The Japanese Banking Crisis

Going by the recent reports, the Japanese banking crisis is not on the verge of getting better. If anything, the situation is deteriorating. Last week’s news indicated that Origami Bank is folding, and today, the reports indicated that Sumo Bank has fallen.

Bonsai Bank, on the other hand, is planning to close some of its branches. The Karaoke Bank has been put up for sale.

The Kamikaze Bank has nose-dived and the Karate Bank is chopping

500 jobs off. Analysts have also indicated that something fishy is going on at the Sushi Bank, and the staff there are afraid they might get a raw deal.

Seeing the Urologist

A man goes to visit a urologist because he has noticed some abnormal growth in his groin area.

Urologist: "It looks like you've got a third testicle growing!"

Man: "Oh... Erm… It isn't that bad, right?

Urologist: "Having a third testicle might have side-effects on your health and on your sexual—"

Man (the man interrupts): "Okay, alright. What can be done?"

Urologist: "Unfortunately, I have neither the expertise nor the equipment to perform a surgery like that one. I'd like to refer you to see another urologist at a clinic. I'll call you a taxi."

Seeing the gravity of the situation, the man is more than grateful for the offer. He takes the taxi and is on his way to the clinic. Sitting in the taxi, tired of the silence, the man decides to break the ice by pulling a joke with the male taxi driver.

Man: "Hey, you know what? There are 5 testicles inside this car."

Confused, the taxi driver turns his head to his passenger and asks, "What? You mean you just got one?"

The Monk, the Priest and the Rabbi

A monk, a priest and a rabbi are seated in a boat. The monk remembers that he left something at the dock and proceeds to run across the water, to the dock, and back. The priest is dumbfounded, seeing the powers of Buddhism. The rabbi doesn't appear moved; he simply nods.

Hours pass an again. This time, the rabbi says he wants to use the bathroom. He proceeds to do just like the monk had done, and runs across the water, getting to the bathroom at the dock. At this point, the priest's mind is blown away, seeing the powers that the two holy men possess.

After some time, the priest himself needs to use the bathroom. He prays to his god and leaps out off the boat into the water. Splash! He falls right into the water. Determined to prove the power of his god, he makes another prayer and tries his luck again. Prayer after prayer, the priest keeps jumping into the water.

Hours later, the priest is already exhausted and drenched with water.

He begins to sob in his defeat. Seeing this, the rabbi leans over to the monk and whispers, "You did tell him about the rocks, right?"

Made In Japan

There happened to be a Japanese who came to America on tour, to see the sights. On his last day in the country, he hailed a cab that would take him to the airport. On the way there, he saw a Honda drive past the taxi. Excited, the man stuck his head out the window and screamed, "Honda! Very fast! Made in Japan."

A few minutes later, a Toyota speeds past the taxi, and again, the Japanese tourist leans out the window and yells, "Toyota! Very fast! Made in Japan."

Another car, a Mitsubishi, sped right past the taxi. Again, the Japanese guy sticks his head out the window and screams again, "Mitsubishi! Very fast! Made in Japan!"

At this time, the driver was fuming mad, but resolved to maintain his calm. The yelling and the leaning, however, continued as a number of cars sped past the taxi.

The driver and his passenger finally get to the airport and read the meter. He announced that the fare read $300. The Japanese guy was shocked. He yelled, "Wah! So expensive!"

The driver screamed back, "Meter! Very fast! Made in Japan!"

The Halloween Party

A couple received an invitation from their family friend to attend a swanky Halloween party. At this party, all attendees were asked to wear masks. Unfortunately, on the material day, the wife was sick, suffering from a terrible headache, and she insisted that her husband attended the party by himself, and to pass her regards to family members he would meet there. Being the doting husband he is, the man objected at first, but after her firm arguments, he decided to go after all. The wife was left taking some aspirin and going to bed. The man took hold of his costume, put it on, and left.

After a sound one-hour nap, the wife suddenly woke up and realized that the pain was all gone. Looking at the clock, she realized that it was still quite early on, and she could still make it to the party. What's more, because her husband was yet to see her costume, and she figured that she might as well have some fun watching how he would react if he thought that she was not around.

In a few minutes, the wife got to the party, and soon enough, she saw her husband in his costume. He was prancing around on the dance floor, getting hold of every beautiful girl he could find, and cupping a part and getting kisses. His wife reached out to him also and being the hot seductive babe herself, the man left the partner he had been with and turned to her. Naturally, since he was her husband, she allowed him to go as far as he wished. A few more drinks and the husband made a proposition in her ear. The lady agreed, and they walked off to one of the cars in the parking lot. They had passionate intercourse in the backseat.

When the couple finished their business, before unmasking, just before midnight, the wife slipped through the crowd and went home. She put away her costumed and climbed into bed. She started thinking about the possible explanation he would make up for this outrageous behavior.

When he came in, the wife was sitting up, reading. She enquired from him the kind of night he had. "Oh, same old thing. You know I never have a good time when you're not there."

"Did you dance much?"

"I tell you, I never danced even one dance. When I got there, I met James, Jude and some other guys, so we went into the spare room and played poker all evening."

"You must have looked quite silly wearing that costume playing poker all night!" she said sarcastically.

"Actually, your brother took over my costume when I arrived at the party. Apparently, he had the time of his life."

The Racist Pilot

A plane at the Los Angeles airport is taking off under the command of a Jewish pilot. Next to him is his Chinese co-pilot, and this is the first flight they are doing together. In the cockpit, there is an awkward silence between the pilots, and they can sense a mutual dislike between them. On reaching the cruising altitude, the pilot sets the plane on autopilot, leans back in his chair and mumbles, "I do not like Chinese!"

"No rike Chinese?" the co-pilot asks, "Why?"

"You people bombed Pearl Harbor, and that's why!" the pilot responds angrily.

"No, no," the Chinese co-pilot objects, "Chinese no bomb Pearl Hahbah. That Japanese, not Chinese."

The pilot answers, "Chinese, Japanese, Vietnamese… Doesn't matter. You're all alike!"

A few quiet moments later, the co-pilot declares, "No rike Jews!"

"Why not?" the pilot wonders.

"Jews let the Titanic sink." The co-pilot says.

"Jews didn't sink the Titanic," the pilot answers. "It was an iceberg."

"Iceberg, Goldberg, Greenberg, Steinberg, Rosenberg, no mattah! All the same!"

Operational Excellence

One time, a Japanese company and an American company went against each other in a competitive boat competition on the Bear River. The two teams practiced long and hard so that they could be at their peak on the day of the performance. When the day came, each team felt more than ready to take on the opponent.

When the race finally happened, the Japanese team won by a mile. The American team was greatly discouraged from the loss and felt their hearts sink.

In a bid to resolve the situation and encourage the team, corporate management decided to look into the matter to explore the possible reason for his crushing defeat. The team chosen to investigate the matter found that the Japanese team had won because it had one person steering and eight others rowing. On the other hand, the American team had eight people steering and one person rowing. The thousands-of-dollars research team found that the issue was that more people had been steering instead of rowing.

In the next year, when the competition came about, the American team was restructured so that there now were three steering directors, three steering managers, and two steering supervisors. Also, the person steering the boat was given a new performance system and accorded more incentives to work harder. It was thought that empowerment and enrichment would do the trick.

To their amazement, in this new year, the Japanese team was ahead by two miles.

Perplexed and embarrassed, the American team's management immediately laid off the rower in a bid to lower its costs and to save up on the cost of the paddles, canceled all ongoing efforts to purchase new capital equipment, and halted the making of a new canoe. However, the consulting firm and the senior executives previously appointed were awarded 'superior performance' awards from the company's savings.

Zen Temple Etiquette

- Do not pee on the tatami, and do not bring your dog, or other pet that could pee on the tatami.

- Do not carry with you any weapons of explosives into the temple unless the head priest authorizes you to.

- Do not replace dry garden stones with erotic statues, even if they are nice.
- Do not draw a mustache on the Buddha image or even glasses, although that makes sense because it would be anachronical.
- Do not tickle a meditating priest, even if you only want to know whether they are faking it or not.
- Do not hold a barbeque or a picnic in the moss gardens, or inside the temple, because it is considered vulgar.
- Do not advertise your commercial products through the loudspeakers, unless there already are loudspeakers from tour guides or recorded explanation of the temple's history. Even for the latter, enquire still from the temple staff, just in case.
- Do not indulge in sexual activities in the Abbot's Hall (there are no specifications for other rooms, although that would also be frowned upon).
- Do not forget to respect the calm and sanctity of the premises.

The Bulldog Eating Mayonnaise

A little boy runs into his house after school and finds his father. He immediately confronts his father, "Dad, I heard the kids at school talking about how awesome a vagina is. What is a vagina, Dad? Have you ever seen it? What does it look like?"

The bewildered father takes a moment to recollect his thoughts before finally saying, "Well, Son, before you use it, it looks like a beautiful flower."

The little boy asks, "How about when you use it?"

The dad grins and asks, "Have you ever seen a bulldog eating mayonnaise?"

The American with an STI

An American man, while traveling across Asia, catches an STI. It all happened after having quite the sexual romp, and he started to see some discoloration and feel discomfort in his groin area. Afraid that he could lose his manhood, the man seeks out a doctor of American origin to get help. The doctor examines his groin area and says, "I'm sorry, it's going to need to be taken out; the disease is too far gone."

The man is understandably shaken, and decides to get a second opinion. Sadly, the next doctor gives him the same diagnosis and solution. Already dismayed, while walking around to process the information, the man sees what appears to be a cultural medicine shop. He is already at the end of his rope and is still in denial, so he goes inside, hoping for a miracle.

Inside, he meets an older gentleman who comes to him. The man explains his situation and the man asks the American to expose his genitals for examination. "Oh, that doesn't look good at all. What did the doctors tell you?" the old guy inquires.

"They said they would have to take it all out," the man responds with disappointment.

Shaking his head, the old man says, "No, no, no… There is no need for that. We need not take it off." The American is excited to hear this, he stands a chance to retain his penis. He starts jumping around screaming with joy. Once seated, he notices that the old man did not rejoice with him, he is just seated there quietly.

"What is the problem? What medicine do you recommend for my dick?"

"I not finish speaking… We need not take it off… Two days tops — it fall off by itself."

Religious Truths

ZEN BUDDHISM: How does shit sound when it's happening?

TAOISM: Shit does happen!

ATHEISTS: There is no apparent reason for shit happening.

PROTESTANTISM: Someone else should get the shit happening to them.

HINDUISM: This shit has recurred!

CONFUCIANISM: Confucius says, "Shit Happens!"

HARE KRISHNA: Shit happens, Shit happens, Happens happens, Shit happens.

AGNOSTICS: Facts happen!

CATHOLICISM: You must have deserved shit if it happens to you.

BUDDHISM: If shit does happen to you, it ain't shit.

EVANGELISTS: Shit will happen to you if you don't send me $5 million

ISLAM: Allah allowed the shit to happen.

CHRISTIAN SCIENTISTS: If shit does happen, it's good.

JUDAISM: Why are we the only ones shit happens to?

JEHOVA'S WITNESSES: If we come in, we can tell you why shit happens.

RASTAFARIANISM: We smoking this shit!

Leprechauns Do Exist!

A man walks into a men's bathroom to take a piss. A few seconds later, while relieving himself, he takes notice of a very short man who walks in and begins peeing in the urinal next to him. Curiosity gets hold of the man, and wanting to see the little fellow, the man looks over the wall separator. To his amazement, the man gets to see the longest girthiest penis he has ever set his eyes on. He mutters to himself, "This short man is surely blessed."

The small man notices the tall man looking at his private parts and starts a casual conversation with him. He says, "I see, you've noticed my penis there, Sir. Do you know why it is so large?"

"No, you tell me," the man replies.

The short guy exclaims, "Can't you see I'm a Leprechaun? And now that you know who I am, I am obliged to give you three wishes. Ask for whatever you wish to have, and it will come to be."

The man gives this statement some thought, but in sarcasm and disbelief says, “Yeah? Sure pal, how about a million dollars? Let’s see if you can make that happen.”

“Piece of cake!” the Leprechaun snaps his finder and continues, “When you arrive home, you will find a suitcase with money on your dinner table. The amount will be $1,000,000.”

The man is now at ease and for his second wish, he asks for a mansion, a great big house. The Leprechaun responds by snapping his fingers then says, “When you return home, your meager crappy house will have vanished, and in its place, you will have a mansion fit for a king.”

The man is now smiling and has a glint in his eye. He says, “Thank you Mr. Leprechaun, thank you.”

The Leprechaun is not ready to let the man go yet.

“Not so fast. You have one more wish, ask for anything you desire.”

The man quickly responds, “I want a hot babe of a wife, a drop dead gorgeous woman with huge cans.”

At the snap of a finger, again, the leprechaun says, “When you get home to your mansion, your new supermodel wife will be donned in a French-maid outfit with her large cleavage bursting from her chest, having prepared a feast and served it for you on the same table your million dollars will be on."

On hearing this, the man is ecstatic! He cannot wait to leave the restroom and head home to meet his three gifts. As he prepares to leave, the leprechaun stops him. "Sir, you cannot leave yet."

"Why not?" the man wonders. "I asked for the three wishes and you granted them to me. I am off to enjoy my new life."

The leprechaun insists, "Alright, but the three wishes come at a cost. If you fail to pay it, you stand to lose the three wishes you made at the snap of my fingers."

"Well, what's the price?" the man asks.

The leprechaun smiles and answers, "You must let me fuck you in the ass until I am satisfied. Do you agree?"

The man is terrified and dumbfounded, especially when he considers the size of the dwarf who wants to violate him. However, he thinks to himself, "Do I give up this new life or do I swallow my pride and allow this leprechaun to violate me?"

… Approximately 30 minutes later…

In the restroom stalls, the man is now crying trying to hold back his pain and tears, however impossible. The leprechaun, on the back, is thrusting and thrusting, exacting the price of the wishes he has granted the man. To take the man's mind off the pain, the leprechaun begins to ask him some questions.

"What is your name, sir?"

"Bob…" The man squeaks.

"Bob, how old are you?"

"45" the man chokes out.

"Bob, you're 45, and you still believe in leprechauns?"

The Holiday in Japan

I went to Japan on holiday and had a close online Japanese friend I had met on the Guitar Hero forum meet me.

I had assumed he was a guy, but to my shock, this really cute girl with short brown hair showed up. I gave her a quick 9 out of 10. Her name was Nao, and although this was the first time we had met in real life, we got along really well.

She revealed to me that she pretends to be a guy online because she wanted to find someone with whom she could speak about rock music because if people realized that she was a girl, they couldn't take her seriously. She apologized, and I quickly told her that I had accepted her apology, but on one condition – that she plays Guitar

Hero with me.

The girl laughed but agreed. I could see her beautiful smile.

We went to her apartment, and she quickly opened her PS4 to access the Guitar Hero. She was a pretty high level, much higher than me, but we played. Somehow, I won. It probably was just luck. The girl turned off the game and began to sulk. She didn't speak to me for a while.

Fearing that our meet-up would end this badly, I leaned over and tried to motivate her.

"Hey Nao, you're a rock star. Get your game on. Go, play…"

The Worst Injury

A guy gets into a terrible accident, and when he is brought to the hospital, he looks down, only to see a bloody rag covering his groin. He also notices that he has lost all feeling in his penis.

Just then, a doctor walks into the room and the guy looks at him and asks, through tears, "Give it to me straight, doctor. How much of it is left?"

"Well," the doctor begins, "If the tattoo you had on read 'Anna,' then you only have a half of it remaining. If it read 'Elena,' then you have two fifths.

The man groans in pain and says, “Doctor, it said ‘Made in Argentina’.”

Naughty Adult Joke Book:
Dirty, Slutty, Funny Jokes That Broke The Censors

Why is a vagina similar to bad weather?

Once it wets, you have to go in.

READ NOW ON AMAZON

Naughty Adult Joke Book #7:
Dirty, Funny And Slutty Jokes That Should Never Be Said In Bed

What makes the cock different from the paycheck?

You never have to beg your wife to blow the paycheck.

READ NOW ON AMAZON.COM

CPSIA information can be obtained
at www.ICGtesting.com
Printed in the USA
LVHW090555261120
672694LV00023B/606

9 781702 916660